W9-AUI-797

The Library of
Turtles and Tortoises ™

Box Turtles

Christopher Blomquist

The Rosen Publishing Group's
PowerKids Press

For Carolyn, a friend to kith and creatures

Published in 2004 by The Rosen Publishing Group, Inc.
29 East 21st Street, New York, NY 10010

First Edition

Editor: Natashya Wilson
Book Design: Michael J. Caroleo
Photo Researcher: Michael J. Caroleo

Photo Credits: Cover and title page © Index Stock Imagery Inc.; p. 4 © Lynn Stone/Animals Animals; pp. 7 (top left), 8 (top), 12 (top), 20 (center) by Bill Beatty; p. 7 (top right) © Tony Wharton; Frank Lane Picture Agency/CORBIS; p. 7 (bottom) © Jonathan Blair/CORBIS; p. 8 (bottom) © Barbara Reed/Animals Animals; pp. 11, 15 (left), 16 (bottom) © Zigmund Leszczynski/Animals Animals; p. 12 (bottom) by Dennis Sheridan; p. 15 (right) © Darren Bennett/Animals Animals; p. 16 (top) © C & E Schwartz/Animals Animals; p. 19 by C. Allen Morgan Photography; p. 20 (top left, top right, bottom right) © Digital Stock; p. 20 (bottom left) © Joe McDonald/CORBIS.

Blomquist, Christopher.
Box turtles / Christopher Blomquist.— 1st ed.
    p. cm. — (The library of turtles and tortoises)
Includes bibliographical references and index.
ISBN 0-8239-6735-2 (lib. bdg.)
1. Terrapene—North America—Juvenile literature. I. Title. II. Series.
QL666.C547 B56 2004
597.92—dc21

                    2002151448

Manufactured in the United States of America

Contents

Plastron

Hinge

Carapace

A Box with Legs

How did the box turtle get its name? As do many turtles, box turtles hide in their shell when they sense danger. Turtles' shells have a top part called a **carapace** and a bottom part called a **plastron**. A box turtle has a bendable place called a **hinge** on its plastron. To hide, the box turtle pulls its head and front legs into the front of its shell and its tail and back legs into the back. Then the plastron bends at the hinge to close the shell. Box turtles close their shells very tightly. Once the shell is closed, it is almost impossible to pry open. When the shell is completely closed, the turtle looks as if it has been sealed inside a box. That is why it is called the box turtle.

This box turtle has closed its shell. The turtle has been turned upside down to show the hinge on its plastron.

A Turtle or a Tortoise?

Some turtles live in freshwater. Other turtles live in the ocean. Some live on land. Tortoises are what people often call **terrestrial** turtles, or turtles that live on land. Scientists agree that true tortoises are a group of turtles that live on land and that have column-shaped hind legs, like an elephant's. Box turtles do live mostly on land, but they do not have column-shaped hind legs, so they are called turtles. They live alone in woods, fields, and swampy areas. Some box turtles swim. As do all turtles, box turtles belong to a group of animals called **reptiles**. Other reptiles include snakes, alligators, and lizards. Reptiles breathe with lungs, have backbones, have scales on their skin, and are **cold-blooded**. Cold-blooded animals need sun to stay warm.

A box turtle's foot (top left) has pointy, fingerlike toes. A desert tortoise (bottom) has column-shaped hind legs that are flat on the bottom, like an elephant's feet (top right).

Turtle and Tortoise Facts

Turtles have been around since the days of the dinosaurs. That's more than 200 million years! Today there are about 270 different types of turtles in the world.

Box Turtle Homes in the United States

Eastern Box Turtles

Box turtles live in North America, China, northern Mexico, and Malaysia. There are two different **species** of box turtle in North America, the ornate box turtle and the eastern box turtle. Adult eastern box turtles have shells that are from 4 to 8 ½ inches (10.2–21.6 cm) long. Their shells are round, like a dome, and are **keeled**. Keeled shells have a raised line running down the middle, which sticks out like a backbone. The shells are brown, black, or green in color. Some eastern box turtles' shells have patterns on them. There are four **subspecies** of eastern box turtle in the United States. One is simply called the eastern box turtle. The other three are the Gulf Coast, the Florida, and the three-toed box turtles. Most three-toed box turtles have three toes on each hind foot, but some have four!

The eastern box turtle (top) has a more colorful shell than does the three-toed box turtle (bottom).

Ornate Box Turtles

The ornate box turtle, also called the western box turtle, is the second species of North American box turtle. There are two subspecies of ornate box turtle, the ornate and the desert ornate. "Ornate" means "highly decorated." The ornate box turtle's shell has a bright pattern on it that is fancier than the eastern box turtle's. The pattern consists of yellow lines on a black or a brown background. An adult ornate box turtle's shell is from 4 to 5 ¾ inches (10.2–14.6 cm) long. The shell is round, but it is not keeled. Some male ornate box turtles are especially pretty. They have green heads and purple tongues! Ornate box turtles are found in the Midwest and the Southwest of the United States and in parts of Mexico. In 1986, Kansas chose the ornate box turtle as its state reptile.

An ornate box turtle, such as this one, has a line running down its back, but the line does not stick up as on a keeled shell.

Turtle and Tortoise Facts

If a turtle eats too much, it will get fat. A turtle is too fat when it can no longer squeeze its body all the way inside its shell.

Come and Get It!

Box turtles have good appetites, but many are picky eaters. They will eat only their favorite types of food. Box turtles are **omnivores**, which means that they eat both meat and plants. Some box turtles also eat **fungi**. Young box turtles often will not eat plants or fungi. They eat worms, insects, slugs, and snails. However, as the turtles grow older, they begin to eat plants, fruits such as berries, and fungi such as mushrooms. Box turtles often feed in the early morning. A box turtle will usually sniff at its food before eating.

Turtles do not have teeth. Instead they use their sharp, heavy jaws to tear food. A turtle's upper jaw hangs over its mouth like a beak.

Box turtles eat small animals, berries, fungi, and seeds. Scientists believe that box turtles may help to spread seeds.

Males, Females, and Mating

It is not always easy to tell male and female box turtles apart. Male box turtles usually have thicker tails than do females. The scales and shell of a male are usually more colorful. Eye color also differs. Male box turtles usually have red eyes. Female box turtles' eyes are usually brown.

Most box turtles mate in the spring or the summer. Box turtles use their sense of smell to find a mate. Each type of box turtle gives off its own odor. To court a female, a male will circle the female and gently bite her shell. When turtles mate, the male, who is normally quiet, may hiss or growl. The male **fertilizes** the female's eggs. A female box turtle can lay fertilized eggs up to three years after she has mated. Some female box turtles will lay eggs whether the eggs have been fertilized or not.

Most male box turtles have red eyes (left). Most female box turtles have brown eyes (right).

Birth and Growth

Female box turtles lay their eggs on land. A mother turtle uses her strong hind legs to dig a nest from 3 to 4 inches (7.6–10.2 cm) deep in soft dirt. She lays from three to eight eggs and buries them. Then she leaves the nest and does not return. Box turtles build nests from May to July. Some ornate box turtles make one nest in May and then dig another nest and lay more eggs in late July. The **temperature** inside the turtle nest must stay around 80°F (26.7°C) for the eggs to **develop**. It takes about three months for the **hatchlings** to be born. Many are born attached to the **yolk sac**, their food source inside the egg. Within a few days, the hatchling absorbs, or takes in, this sac, and the baby turtle begins to eat solid food. Hatchlings born in the fall may stay in their underground nests until spring.

A mother box turtle (top) lays her eggs in a dirt nest. Baby box turtles (bottom) become fully grown in about 20 years.

Asleep for the Winter

Wintry weather is not good for box turtles. As do all cold-blooded creatures, box turtles need warmth to heat their bodies and to stay healthy. Their favorite foods, bugs and fresh plants, are not easy to find in the winter. To stay alive during this time, some box turtles **hibernate**, or go to sleep. During hibernation, a turtle does not eat. It uses stored body fat for energy. To hibernate, box turtles bury themselves in the ground. Some dig down as far as 5 ½ feet (1.7 m). Being underground protects the turtle from frost, ice, and snow. Turtles wake from hibernation in the spring.

Not all box turtles hibernate. Box turtles that live in places where the weather stays above 64°F (17.8°C) in the winter may stay active. Others may nap for a few days or weeks.

To hibernate, most box turtles will dig a den such as this one into the dirt of a riverbank or a hillside.

Turtle and Tortoise Facts

Hibernating box turtles sometimes dig deeper into their hibernation dens as the weather gets colder at the surface. Although box turtles usually live alone, they sometimes hibernate in groups.

Enemies and Danger

A box turtle's strong shell cannot save the turtle from all its enemies. Animals such as foxes, skunks, raccoons, opossums, large birds, dogs, and snakes eat box turtles. Most eat the eggs or the hatchlings. Adult box turtles are hard to kill, but they can be hurt by these **predators**. If a box turtle's shell gets cracked, the turtle inside is no longer as safe as it was. Box turtles are also in danger if they tip over and cannot right themselves.

Humans are another danger to box turtles. People once hunted box turtles for food. Today people do not eat box turtles, but cars and farmers' plows sometimes run over box turtles by accident. Other box turtles are taken from the wild and are sold as pets.

Box turtles can get into trouble if they tip over, but usually they are able to right themselves, as did this turtle (center). Box turtle predators include racoons, opossums, dogs, and snakes.

Long-Lived Pets

Healthy box turtles can live a long time. The **life span** of most box turtles is anywhere from 30 to 75 years. A few box turtles are known to have lived more than 100 years.

The box turtle is one of the most popular types of pet turtle. Some box turtles can learn to know their owner's voice and will come when they are called! Only box turtles that have been raised in **captivity** should be kept as pets. In many places, it is against the law to take box turtles from the wild.

Pet box turtles can be fun, but they are also a lot of work. Box turtles need the right food, care, and clean space to live in or they may get sick. Before you get a pet box turtle, be sure that you can take care of it properly. Remember, inside that box of a shell is an amazing, living creature!

Glossary

captivity (kap-TIH-vih-tee) A place where animals live, such as in a home, a zoo, or an aquarium, instead of living in the wild.

carapace (KER-uh-pays) The upper part of a turtle's shell.

cold-blooded (KOHLD-bluh-did) Having a body heat that changes with the surrounding heat.

develop (dih-VEH-lup) To grow or expand.

fertilizes (FUR-tih-ly-ziz) Puts male cells inside a female to make babies.

fungi (FUN-jy) Living things that are like plants but that don't have leaves, flowers, or green color, and that don't make their own food.

hatchlings (HACH-lingz) Baby animals that have just come out of their shells.

hibernate (HY-bur-nayt) To spend the winter in a sleeplike state.

hinge (HINJ) A bendable part.

keeled (KEELD) Having a raised line running down the center.

life span (LYF SPAN) The amount of time that something is alive.

omnivores (OM-nih-vorz) Animals that eat both plants and animals.

plastron (PLAS-tron) The bottom, flatter part of a turtle's shell that covers the belly.

predators (PREH-duh-terz) Animals that kill other animals for food.

reptiles (REP-tylz) Cold-blooded animals with lungs and scales. Turtles, snakes, and lizards are reptiles.

species (SPEE-sheez) A single kind of plant or animal.

subspecies (SUB-spee-sheez) Types within a species.

temperature (TEM-pruh-chur) How hot or cold something is.

terrestrial (tuh-RES-tree-ul) Living on land.

yolk sac (YOHK SAK) A baglike part inside an egg that holds the yolk, the liquid that feeds the growing baby animal.

Index

C
carapace, 5
China, 9
cold-blooded, 6, 18

D
desert ornate box turtle, 10

E
eastern box turtle(s), 9
eggs, 14, 17, 21
enemies, 21
eyes, 14

F
female, 14, 17
Florida box turtle, 9
food(s), 13, 18, 21
fungi, 13

G
Gulf Coast box turtle, 9

H
hatchlings, 17, 21
hibernation, 18

L
life span, 22

M
Malaysia, 9
male, 14
mate, 14
Mexico, 9–10

N
nest, 17
North America, 9

O
odor, 14
omnivores, 13
ornate box turtle, 9–10

P
pet(s), 21–22
plastron, 5

R
reptile(s), 6, 10

S
shell, 5, 10, 14, 21

T
three-toed box turtle, 9
tortoises, 6

Web Sites

Due to the changing nature of Internet links, PowerKids Press has developed an online list of Web sites related to the subject of this book. This list is updated regularly. Please use this link to access the list:
www.powerkidslinks.com/ltt/box/